GW00503816

ON YOUR
RETIREMENT

ON YOUR RETIREMENT

Summersdale Publishers Ltd
46 West Street
Chichester
West Sussex
PO19 1RP
UK

www.summersdale.com

Printed and bound in China

ISBN: 978-1-84953-421-5

TO............................
FROM........................

The future belongs to those who believe in the beauty of their dreams.

ELEANOR ROOSEVELT

May you live
all the days
of your life.

JONATHAN SWIFT

Whatever you
can do, or dream
you can do, begin
it. Boldness has
genius, power, and
magic in it.

W. H. MURRAY

The trouble with
retirement is
that you never
get a day off.

ABE LEMONS

Not a shred of
evidence exists in
favour of the idea that
life is serious.

BRENDAN GILL

You are only
young once,
but you can
stay immature
indefinitely.

OGDEN NASH

A WISE man will MAKE

MORE
opportunities
than he
FINDS.

FRANCIS BACON

I HAVE FOUND THAT IF
YOU LOVE LIFE, LIFE
WILL LOVE YOU BACK.

ARTHUR RUBINSTEIN

Don't simply retire
from something; have
something to retire to.

HARRY EMERSON FOSDICK

My idea of
hell is to
be young
again.

MARGE PIERCY

Be happy while y'er leevin, for y'er a lang time deid.

SCOTTISH PROVERB

You and I possess
within ourselves,
at every moment of
our lives, under all
circumstances, the
power to transform
the quality of our
lives.

WERNER ERHARD

First say to yourself
what you would be;
and then do what you
have to do.

EPICTETUS

Some run swiftly; some creep painfully; all who keep on will reach the goal.

PIYADASSI MAHA THERA

IT IS RIGHT TO
BE CONTENTED
WITH WHAT WE
HAVE, BUT NEVER
WITH WHAT WE ARE.

JAMES MACKINTOSH

Better than a hundred years of IDLENESS

is one day
spent in
DETERMINATION.

SIDDHĀRTHA GAUTAMA BUDDHA

To succeed in life, you need three things: a wishbone, a backbone and a funny bone.

REBA MCENTIRE

Life is a progress, and not a station.

RALPH WALDO EMERSON

Let life happen to you. Believe me, life is in the right, always.

RAINER MARIA RILKE

Nobody can go back
and start a new
beginning, but anyone
can start today and
make a new ending.

MARIA ROBINSON

Learn from yesterday, live for today, hope for tomorrow. The important thing is not to stop questioning.

ALBERT EINSTEIN

Life isn't about finding yourself. Life is about creating yourself.

GEORGE BERNARD SHAW

Retirement is
WONDERFUL
if you have two
ESSENTIALS –

much to

LIVE ON

and much to

LIVE FOR.

ANONYMOUS

YOU CAN'T TURN BACK
THE CLOCK BUT YOU
CAN WIND IT UP AGAIN.

BONNIE PRUDDEN

The diamond cannot be polished without friction, nor the man perfected without trials.

CHINESE PROVERB

The past is
a guidepost,
not a
hitching
post.

L. THOMAS HOLDCROFT

Whatever with the past has gone, the best is always yet to come.

LUCY LARCOM

Youth is the
gift of nature,
but age is a
work of art.

GARSON KANIN

You only live once,
but if you do it right,
once is enough.

MAE WEST

One man in his
time plays
many parts.

WILLIAM SHAKESPEARE

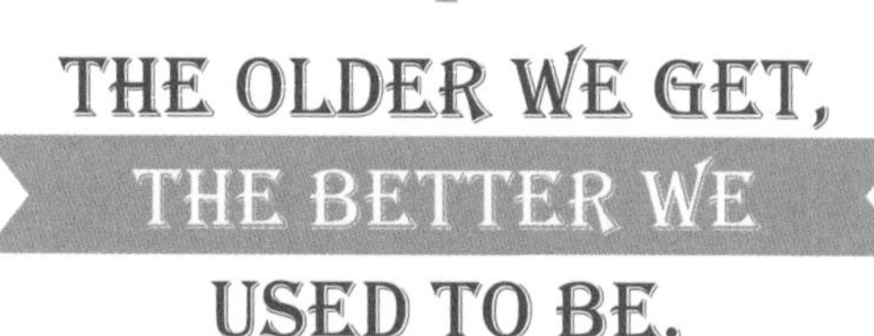

THE OLDER WE GET,
THE BETTER WE
USED TO BE.

ANONYMOUS

The
GOLDEN
age is
BEFORE
us,

not
BEHIND
us.

SALLUST

Live each day as if it
were your last, and
garden as though you
will live forever.

ANONYMOUS

Life has got
to be lived –
that's all
there is
to it.

ELEANOR ROOSEVELT

Retirement at 65 is ridiculous. When I was 65 I still had pimples.

GEORGE BURNS

If you enjoy living,
it is not difficult
to keep the sense
of wonder.

RAY BRADBURY

People are always asking about the good old days. I say, why don't you say the good now days?

ROBERT M. YOUNG

A little nonsense now and then, is relished by the wisest men.

ROALD DAHL

When they tell me I'm **TOO OLD** to do something,

I attempt it

IMMEDIATELY.

PABLO PICASSO

THE KEY TO
SUCCESSFUL AGEING
IS TO PAY AS LITTLE
ATTENTION TO IT AS
POSSIBLE.

JUDITH REGAN

Men are like wine.
Some turn to vinegar,
but the best improve
with age.

POPE JOHN XXIII

To me, old age is always 15 years older than I am.

BERNARD BARUCH

Let us celebrate the occasion with wine and sweet words.

PLAUTUS

Seize the moment. Remember all those women on the *Titanic* who waved off the dessert cart.

ERMA BOMBECK

When you get to retirement, you switch bosses – from the one who hired you to the one who married you.

GENE PERRET

I don't want to retire. I'm not that good at crossword puzzles.

NORMAN MAILER

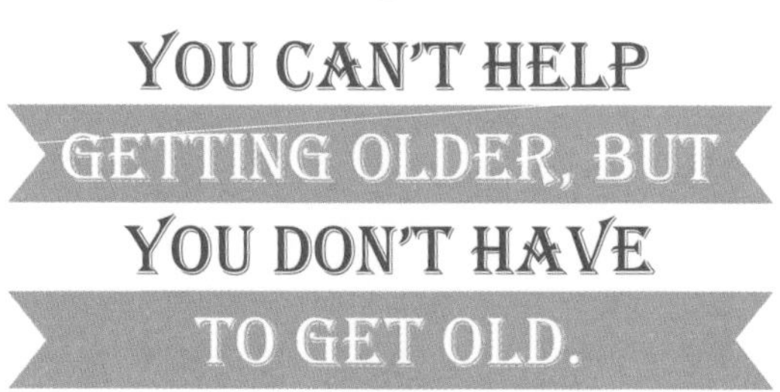

YOU CAN'T HELP
GETTING OLDER, BUT
YOU DON'T HAVE
TO GET OLD.

GEORGE BURNS

If you want
a thing done
WELL,

get a couple of OLD BROADS to do it.

BETTE DAVIS

Retire from work,
but not from life.

ANONYMOUS

If you obey
all the rules,
you will miss
all the
fun.

KATHARINE HEPBURN

We do not stop playing because we grow old. We grow old because we stop playing.

BENJAMIN FRANKLIN

Do not worry about avoiding temptation. As you grow older it will avoid you.

JOEY ADAMS

Oh, to be 70 again.

GEORGES CLEMENCEAU, ON SEEING A PRETTY GIRL ON HIS 80TH BIRTHDAY

To get back my youth I would do anything in the world, except take exercise, get up early, or be respectable.

OSCAR WILDE

Growing old is
COMPULSORY,

growing up is
OPTIONAL.

BOB MONKHOUSE

MY ONLY REGRET
IN LIFE IS THAT I
DIDN'T DRINK MORE
CHAMPAGNE.

JOHN MAYNARD KEYNES

I'm not interested in age. People who tell me their age are silly. You're as old as you feel.

ELIZABETH ARDEN

You don't get older, you get better.

SHIRLEY BASSEY

Retirement is wonderful. It's doing nothing without worrying about getting caught at it.

GENE PERRET

You're never too old to become younger.

MAE WEST

They say that age is all in your mind. The trick is keeping it from creeping down into your body.

ANONYMOUS

How pleasant is the day when we give up striving to be young – or slender.

WILLIAM JAMES

I'M 63 NOW, BUT THAT'S JUST 17 CELSIUS.

GEORGE CARLIN

The **OLDER**
you get, the
BETTER
you get –

unless
you're a
BANANA.

ANONYMOUS

How old would you
be if you didn't know
how old you were?

SATCHEL PAIGE

Looking 50 is great – if you're 60.

JOAN RIVERS

One of the best parts of growing older? You can flirt all you like since you've become harmless.

LIZ SMITH

To keep the heart
unwrinkled, to be
hopeful, kindly,
cheerful, reverent
– that is to triumph
over old age.

THOMAS BAILEY ALDRICH

Beautiful young people are accidents of nature, but beautiful old people are works of art.

ELEANOR ROOSEVELT

When a man retires and time is no longer a matter of urgent importance, his colleagues generally present him with a watch.

R. C. SHERRIFF

How BEAUTIFUL it is to do NOTHING,

and then
to **REST**
afterward.

SPANISH PROVERB

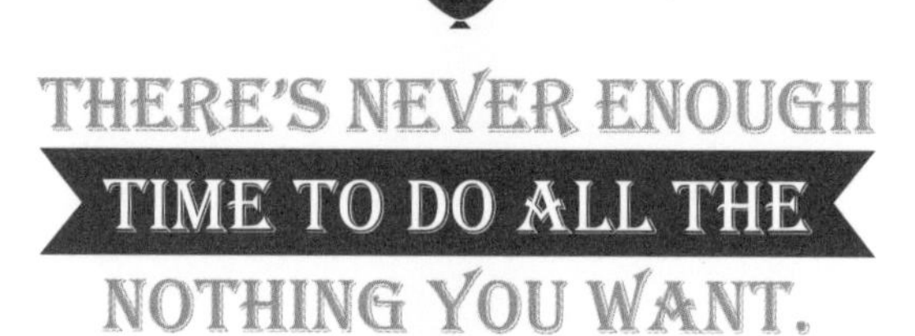

THERE'S NEVER ENOUGH
TIME TO DO ALL THE
NOTHING YOU WANT.

BILL WATTERSON

If people concentrated
on the really
important things
in life, there'd be a
shortage of fishing
poles.

DOUG LARSON

Every man is the architect of his own fortune.

APPIUS CLAUDIUS CAECUS

Age is not a particularly interesting subject. Anyone can get old. All you have to do is live long enough.

GROUCHO MARX

Age is only a
number, a cipher
for the records.
A man can't retire
his experience.
He must use it.

BERNARD BARUCH

What do gardeners do when they retire?

BOB MONKHOUSE

How blest is he
who crowns, in
shades like these,
A youth of labour
with an age of
ease!

OLIVER GOLDSMITH

TAKE REST; A
FIELD THAT HAS
RESTED GIVES A
BOUNTIFUL CROP.

OVID

It's SAD

to grow old,

but NICE
to RIPEN.

BRIGITTE BARDOT

Age is just a number. It's totally irrelevant unless, of course, you happen to be a bottle of wine.

JOAN COLLINS

I haven't matured,
progressed, grown,
become deeper,
wiser, or funnier.
But then, I never
thought I would.

PETER COOK